Marcelo Nogueira

Proportionality in Tax Substitution for Presumed Taxable Events

Marcelo Nogueira

Proportionality in Tax Substitution for Presumed Taxable Events

ScienciaScripts

Imprint

Cover image: www.ingimage.com

This book is a translation from the original published under ISBN 978-620-2-03435-7.

Publisher:
Sciencia Scripts
is a trademark of
Dodo Books Indian Ocean Ltd. and OmniScriptum S.R.L publishing group

120 High Road, East Finchley, London, N2 9ED, United Kingdom
Str. Armeneasca 28/1, office 1, Chisinau MD-2012, Republic of Moldova, Europe
Managing Directors: Ieva Konstantinova, Victoria Ursu
info@omniscriptum.com

Printed at: see last page
ISBN: 978-620-8-37645-1

To my beloved Ana Claudia, Carolina and Helena, who have given new and wonderful meaning to my life, making me a better man every day.

SUMMARY

The aim of this paper is to discuss the theory of forward tax substitution for a presumed taxable event, elaborating a description of the application of the law, in which the individual guarantee of the ability to pay is related to the public interest in making taxation operationally viable. The methodological premises of the theory of principles will be analyzed, as will the model for applying proportionality to the normative species and the structure and content of the right to the ability to pay in the face of the rules on forward tax substitution. The methodological premise will be that expressed in the judgment of Direct Unconstitutionality Action No. 1.851-4/AL, i.e. the competence granted by paragraph 7 of art. 150 of the CRFB, which determines an indirect taxation regime with definitive incidence in the early part of economic cycles, without being interpreted as anticipation, preventing refunds in the event that the actual taxable events have lower values than those presumed. The method used will be bibliographical research, comparing doctrine and case law, accessed in periodicals, books and on the website of the Federal Supreme Court. In the context of constitutional theories and legal philosophy, analysis will be carried out in order to establish the premises of the general theory of law. The discourse will be expository-argumentative and the research will be a monograph of theoretical analysis using the rational method. This work will analyze the possibilities for giving greater fiscal justice to the legal-tax treatment of the issue.

SUMMARY

INTRODUCED

Tax substitution is a typical collection technique for multi-stage taxes on consumption, through which the occurrence of one of the stages in the economic cycle of a given good creates the presumption that the subsequent stages will occur towards the final consumer.

Thus, the obligation to pay the tax is based on the economic expression that the product is presumed to have, without taking into account the actual value of the transactions, but rather the presumed value.

The most classic example of this type of situation is the ICMS (tax on the movement of goods) on the sale of cars from the industry to the end consumer. In this hypothesis, the value of the legal transactions in this chain is estimated and the tax becomes due in full at the time of the first sales transaction (e.g. from the manufacturer to the distributor) based on the value that it is assumed will be sold to the final consumer at the end of the chain.

This instrument, which aims to make tax collection more practical, was introduced into our legal system by Amendment No. 3 to the Federal Constitution, enacted on March 17, 1993.

For many years, the conformity of this Amendment to the Constitution was questioned, but at the end of 2002, the Federal Supreme Court ruled that it was constitutional in Direct Unconstitutionality Action No. 1.851-4/AL. However, even after this decision, the amendment continued to be questioned.

However, this constitutional provision is an exception to the fundamental right to pay taxes in accordance with one's ability to pay, as it authorizes taxation based on approximate values in order to make collection feasible, which would otherwise be excessively onerous and extremely difficult, if not almost impossible.

Under the lens of proportionality, it is possible to verify the compatibility of this exception to a fundamental right with our constitutional tax system. Even the Supreme Court, in declaring the constitutionality of the technique of forward tax substitution for a presumed taxable event, did not do so without limit. And the idea of this work is to point out the necessary limits so that the principles involved are weighted with due proportionality.

For this reason, the aforementioned judgment has been taken as the methodological premise of this work. It is assumed that the aforementioned constitutional provision authorizes the indirect taxation system with incidence on the beginning of economic cycles in a definitive manner, i.e. it is not a mere anticipation. Thus, if the taxable event actually occurs has a lower tax base than the presumed tax base, the amounts will not be refunded.

It will thus be shown how this tax regime interferes with the guarantee of the ability to pay so that the weighing up of values carried out by the derived constituent power does not descend into the total discretion of the legislator, to the extent that this regime must be accompanied by a proper demonstration of the specific scope so that the balancing act carried out by the constitutional reformer proves to be appropriate.

In this sense, it is necessary to study definitions of the methodological premises of the theory of principles and the proportionality model, as well as to analyze the structure and content of the principle of contributory capacity.

The method used will be bibliographical research, comparing doctrine and case law, accessed in periodicals, books and on the website of the Federal Supreme Court. There will also be recourse to comparative law, with due caution in not importing conclusions that are different from the circumstances, paying attention to the positive law of each state. In the context of constitutional theories and legal philosophy, analysis will take place in order to establish the premises of the general theory of law.

The discourse will be expository-argumentative and the research will be of the type of monograph of theoretical analysis in the rational method.

Finally, through all these methodological aspects, the aim is to contribute to the realization of tax justice.

By virtue of Constitutional Amendment No. 3/93, Article 150 of the Constitution of the Federative Republic of Brazil now includes paragraph 7, which establishes forward or progressive tax substitution by presumed taxable event. Forward tax substitution is a typical collection technique for multi-phase taxes on consumption, such as the ICMS (Tax on the Circulation of Goods and Services). Under this technique, the occurrence of one of the stages of the economic cycle presupposes the occurrence of the others up to the final consumer. With each operation, the value of the legal business is estimated and the respective tax becomes due in full on the first operation based on the final value of the sale to the end consumer. The consequence is that a presumption of economic expression is used as the basis for calculating the tax, to the detriment of the actual value of the transactions. This raises questions about the justification for taxing an actual taxable event that is lower than the presumed taxable event and how to combine the guarantee of the ability to pay with the technique of forward tax substitution on presumed taxable events. Finally, the impact of proportionality on the dialogue of sources between the ability to pay and the operationality of tax collection in the face of the forward tax substitution technique on presumed taxable events is analyzed.

The principle of the ability to pay is violated and the tax rule needs to be weighed against the constitutional guarantee through proportionality. Even though the Supreme Court has considered this incidence to be constitutional, this does not mean that the legislature has broad freedom to set up forward tax substitution schemes.

CHAPTER 1
THEORY OF PRINCIPLES AND ABILITY TO PAY

1.1 The definition of the legal principle

By considering the presumed value of the legal transaction as the calculation basis, the tax substitution system for the presumed taxable event can restrict the guarantee of paying taxes in accordance with the ability to pay. For this reason, it is necessary to clearly define what is meant by the principle.

Since law is a cultural construct, its rules are directly related to the values that the society that produces it expresses or seeks to express. Values such as Justice and Social Peace, for example, have different conceptions that vary according to the reality of each nation. However, it is possible to distinguish a common essence, especially when the nations in question are influenced by the same roots as their normative texts, as is the case with European and Latin American countries.

When the law includes these values in its norms, whether as principles or rules, it makes it possible to clearly distinguish values from legal norms because, while values act in the field of morality, stating that something is valid, legal norms state what it should be.

1.1.1 Distinctions based on the generality and abstraction of norms

Positive law is made up of norms, which can be classified as rules or principles. At first, the aim was to demonstrate the normativity of principles, in order to explain judicial decisions based not only on normative texts. Subsequently, the need arose for criteria to be established objectively in order to provide more consistency in the grounds for interpretation and application based on principles.

The term principle is vague and ambiguous, as pointed out by PONTES (2000), for whom, by articulating the legal-positive order around principles that give organic systematicity to the actual functioning of the law, there is a profound change in the way we think about and apply the law.

The Enlightenment movement, in turn, signaled a need for certainty, objectivity and simplicity, summarizing the interpretation and application of the law as the operation of a syllogism. Montesquieu stated that "the judge is the mouth of the law". Rousseau would refer to the general will as an intrinsic part of the generality of norms.

The notions of generality and abstraction, according to this author, were also aimed at the security and stability of human relations. However, since law is ontologically made up of vague and ambiguous expressions and interpreted by people, there is no denying its aspect as a "plane of reality" and a "historically situated cultural manifestation", relegating the Enlightenment ideal of rationality and generalization to the field of utopias.

Faced with the reality of principles, the idea of syllogism is abandoned and the concept of the construction of the legal norm applicable to the specific case is adopted. The principles, then, would come to affirm, in a constitution, the fundamental values, objectives and desires of a given society.

1.1.2 Evolution of structural distinctions

In 1956, Esser defined principle *(Grundsatz)* as the direct or indirect way in which normative prescriptions are established (AVILA, 1999), abandoning the circles of generality and abstraction.

DWORKIN (1977) made a distinction between guidelines, principles and rules, according to which the former would be objectives of an economic, social or political nature. Principles would be inescapable requirements of "justice, loyalty or any other moral aspect", establishing rights. Rules, then, would contain the description of a fact, its consequences and its exceptions. The principles would constitute a reason to decide weighed against other reasons derived from other principles. Thus, rules would be applied in full or not at all, while principles would have a dimension according to the specific case. According to this author, principles have a dimension of weight or importance that rules do not. Rules cannot have this dimension of weight because, if there is a conflict between rules, one must necessarily be invalidated and the conflict resolved by other rules, such as those based on the criteria of hierarchy, chronology and specialty.

The so-called "new constitutional interpretation" is not restricted to the subsumptive method, so that the meaning of the rule can be defined in the light of the specific case, its factual circumstances and the principles involved. The principles, then, would be norms that identify values that must be preserved or ends that are sought. Rules, on the other hand, would only describe conduct. Thus, norms would be descriptions of conduct and principles would be evaluative or finalistic.

ALEXY (2001) made a distinction that was more coherent and clearer. Agreeing with DWORKIN (1977), he states that the law expresses its commands through principles and rules, disagreeing with the use of generality as a distinguishing criterion insofar as he considers rules and principles to be types of norm because they precept a must-be. For ALEXY (2001), principles are rules that order something to be done to the greatest extent possible within the existing legal and factual possibilities, and there are therefore different degrees of compliance with principles. Rules, on the other hand, are complied with or not. They establish definitive duties and, in the event of conflict with others of the same kind, they represent judgments of duty to be that contradict each other, resolved by the introduction of an exception clause or by criteria of validity (specialty, chronology and hierarchy). In a collision of principles, one gives way to the other, without any exceptionality or invalidity.

For SIECKMANN (2006), principles are reasons to be weighed up and weighings are rational decision-making processes in the application of the law and contain the foundation of a relationship of pre-eminence established between two colliding principles. The principle would lead to the realization of a content, interfering in the weighting, but the principle alone would establish what should be complied with in all cases, as a prima *facie* obligation. The author proposes an alternative model called the model of interaction of mandates of validity. The distinction between principles and rules, based on the *prima facie* criterion, is criticized by

AVILA (2008) because it lies in the different potential that normative species have for decision-making, with rules having a greater potential for deciding issues because they directly describe conduct, as well as requiring a greater argumentative burden in order to be dismissed.

AVILA (2008) proposes as the main distinguishing criteria the way in which they describe conduct and ends. Rules would be norms that directly describe conduct and indirectly describe ends. Principles would be norms that directly describe ends and indirectly describe conduct.

1.1.3 The dual nature of some legal provisions

For DWORKIN (1977), rules and principles could fulfill the same role, varying only in form, but what is observed is that they have different contents, as in the case of the rule of legality and the principle of legality.

AVILA (2008) points out that the same textual provision can generate norms with the structure of a principle and a rule. In this sense, the requirement of a law in the formal sense for taxes to be levied is a rule, which is not complied with to a greater or lesser degree. Either the rule is complied with, by instituting the tax through a law in the formal sense, and the tax is valid. Or the rule is not complied with and the tax is not valid.

However, the command that states that, as far as possible, the tax incidence rules contain all aspects of the hypothesis of incidence is a principle, a typical optimization commandment, which is not fulfilled objectively. From this point of view, the principle of legality seeks legal certainty, but in practice it can come into conflict with the generality and abstraction of the tax rules, which aim to make them practicable and thus achieve tax justice.

1.1.4 The structural distinction between principles and rules and their resistance

The concept of principle and its differences from rules is a subject that has yet to be settled. In the tax field, MACHADO (2004), following in the footsteps of BANDEIRA DE MELLO (2007), still maintains that principles are hierarchically superior legal norms with a greater degree of abstraction and generality than rules.

CARVALHO (2005) lists various categories of legal principles, emphasizing that they do not form part of positive law, as they do not have a linguistic formation with a syntactic structure. According to the author, principles only constitute a strong axiological charge, since only legal norms are part of positive law. For him, principles are rules that carry significant nuclei of great magnitude, influencing the normative chains to which they grant a character of relative unity. In short, principles would have an aggregating function for other rules in the positive system and, therefore, there would be no distinction between norms and principles.

1.1.5 Problems of resistance to the structural distinction between principles and rules

The risk of not distinguishing between legal principles and rules is that the protection of fundamental rights is undermined because the broad scope of principles prevents them from being interpreted as rules. In many cases, the Constitution determines the maximum application of certain rights, without precisely defining the limits.

This is why the structural distinction between principles and rules aims to guarantee the greatest possible effectiveness for the fundamental rights guaranteed through principles. While rules determine definitive duties, in a hypothesis-consequence relationship, applied by subsumption, principles establish *primafacie* duties, which must be tirelessly pursued by the state.

Since the limits of state intervention in a fundamental right are at the heart of this work, it is important to define and detail which fundamental right we are talking about and the possibilities for restricting it.

1.2 The fundamental right to respect for the ability to pay as a principle

1.2.1 Origin and general notions

UCKMAR (1999) states that the first signs of taxation occurred among the Sumdrians, in the territory now occupied by Iraq. By 2000 BC, the Egyptians were already paying direct and indirect taxes.

The ability to pay, in turn, appears in the science of finance as the suitability of assets to participate in public charges. The vagueness of this concept has been criticized by various scholars, with COSTA (1991) going so far as to state that it would be necessary to adopt a definition that is sufficiently general to be acceptable to all.

GIARDINA (1961) defines it as the susceptibility to bear the tax burden, the suitability to pay tax, the possibility of being the subject of the public entity's demand, keeping in this concept gaps that can be filled by any content.

In the midst of the endless debate, the idea that it would be the contribution according to fiscal aptitude, corresponding to tax justice itself, was accepted with a certain tranquillity.

In Brazil, COSTA (2003) distinguished three levels of definition of the issue: a) the subjection of the individual to obligations and the ownership of rights based on the law; b) the economic aptitude of the subject to bear or be the recipient of taxes and; c) the possession or use of wealth, easily identifiable and in a situation presumably sufficient to bear the tax.

It should be noted that there is a rule and a principle relating to the ability to pay, which are distinct fundamental rights.

1.2.2 From the rule to the principle of ability to pay

According to BARRETO (1998), our Constitution defines contributory capacity in objective and subjective terms. The first is translated as the act-fact, fact or state of fact connected to the taxpayer that reveals an economic content ontologically considered, without subjective considerations.

Considering the ability to pay as a material aspect of the hypothesis of incidence, we are talking about a definitive duty, which is fulfilled or not. It is a rule of fundamental law, with antecedent and consequent, with an express obligation to behave. The legislator is forbidden to establish, as a taxable event, any aspect that is not an indicator of contributory capacity. This is what is enshrined in Article 145, §1 of the Constitution, which states that taxes shall comply with the ability to pay.

However, the commandment to keep within the limits of effective wealth as much as possible is not absolute, but neither can the legislator depart from it for mere convenience; it is necessary to justify it and present a basis in rules of the same hierarchy.

1.2.3 The tax base as the "only" numerical expression of the taxable event

A considerable number of scholars do not accept the idea that the legislator has the option of defining the tax base for taxes and contributions, envisioning a second rule whereby the definition of the tax base must be as detailed as possible, as if there were only one possible definition to accurately reflect the taxable event. The contributory capacity that functions as a constitutional circle would be the subjective capacity of each individual.

However, this view fails to resolve a number of issues and does not ensure the effectiveness of the fundamental right it prescribes because individual contributory capacity should not be the absolute criterion for quantifying taxes, even if it is linked to the definition of the most detailed and subjective calculation basis possible.

1.2.4 The options for the calculation basis are at the legislator's discretion in compliance with the principle of the "tax base".

When defining the tax base, it is important to ask what the economic object of taxation is and who should definitely pay the tax and in what way, according to the legislator's intention.

The legislator must first observe the rules of jurisdiction and, in addition, he must always use, among the calculation bases he has, the one that makes it possible to better individualize the graduation of the tax in relation to the ability to pay.

1.2.5 The possibility of weighing up the principle of ability to pay

Observing the ability to pay entails choosing only the taxable events that are indicative of this ability, as a rule, as well as establishing a tax base that represents the measure of that event as accurately as possible.

In the case of fiscal and extra-fiscal functions, we note the presence of two principles to be weighed up, one guaranteeing a fundamental right and the other a collective interest. These categories cannot be confused, just as it is not possible to equate constitutional duties with fundamental rights. There are no fundamental duties with the same normative structure, scope of protection and broad factual support as fundamental rights. The collective interest cannot justify all kinds of restrictions on fundamental rights. To do so, it must be expressed by means of a constitutional principle, there must be an imposition in the Constitution of an ideal state of affairs that justifies such restrictions.

CHAPTER 2
THE CONTENT OF THE ABILITY TO PAY PRINCIPLE

2.1 The ability to pay as a criterion of equality in taxes and contributions with a taxable event

In relation to taxation, there are different constitutional principles that can sometimes clash. Recalling the need to optimize axiological commands, it is recommended that the principles should coexist with the minimum possible intervention of one against the other.

In this context, the practicability of taxation, as an expression of the collective interest, will clash with the guarantee of the ability to pay. Since taxation limits the rights to freedom and property, it is necessary to identify what other constitutionally protected interests it is intended to stimulate. To do this, it is necessary to understand the various functions that tax rules can take on.

2.1.1 The functions of tax rules

Лкчп of the fiscal function, referring to the collection of revenue to cover state expenses, taxation also performs the extra-fiscal, economic or social policy functions, and the simplifying function, governed by the principle of practicability in the sense of adopting global measures to simplify the tax system.

However, these functions do not fall exclusively to the rules. The same rule that has an extra-fiscal function may also have a fiscal function, albeit in a subsidiary way. As KRAKOWIAK (2005) points out, there is no tax rule marked by a single function in an absolute way. However, given the overwhelming predominance of one function over the others, the criterion is important.

In the case of tax rules of a fiscal nature, what differentiates taxpayers is the ability to pay, and it is reasonable to conceive that this is not a principle, but a criterion of distinction for the promotion of equality. What makes it possible to move from formal equality to material equality in tax law is the ability to pay.

TORRES (2007) sees taxation as a guarantee of fundamental freedoms because, as a fundamental duty, it arises in the space opened up by those freedoms and is totally limited by them. For this author, the roots of taxation are to be found in sections XXII and XXIII of Article 5 of the Constitution, which proclaims the right to property and freedom of initiative. The ability to pay would be the cause of taxes, the consideration the cause of fees and the expense or public work the cause of contributions.

TIPKE and LANG (2008) state, however, that the study of the justification or cause of taxes, in the science of finance, makes it possible to draw up rational criteria for taxes, avoiding arbitrariness in the legislative activity of creating and drawing up taxes.

2.1.2 The search for the cause and the definition of principles as a criterion of equality

Despite the criticism of TORRES (2007), it is feasible to analyze the cause of taxes, such as their justification, in order to, from this aspect, define the primary functions of the tax rule and the principles that will be adopted in the distribution of the tax burden.

The principle of equality requires the consistent adoption of comparison criteria to identify those in an equivalent situation. In this context, the ability to pay comes to be the comparison criterion in taxation with a primarily fiscal function. Thus, the legislator must use this criterion, unless there is some aspect that justifies it on the basis of constitutional norms that also establish *prima facie* duties, such as free competition and environmental protection.

Thus, tax equality, from the point of view of the fair distribution of the tax burden, is achieved through the maximum use of the ability to pay as a distinguishing criterion.

2.1.3 The dimensions of justice and equality

The principle of equality is only fully realized when it is conceived in both its formal and material dimensions. If one of these dimensions is missing, there is no justice because it cannot be absolutely individual, otherwise the abstraction and generality of the law will be violated.

Optimizing equality in the law will allow taxes to be created according to each person's ability to pay. On the other hand, there is no point in having extreme equality on the material level of the law if the application does not follow this equality because it becomes impractical under the formal level of the law.

This is why it is essential to balance the ability to pay against practicality when drafting laws.

At this point, it should be noted that principles do not only convey fundamental (individual) rights, but also collective goods, such as efficiency in taxation, usually referred to as practicability or practicality.

2.2 Subjective and objective aspects of taxation according to ability to pay

2.2.1 Traditional distinctions between absolute/objective relative/subjective ability to pay

GIARDINA (1961) points out that, at first, the application of the ability to pay is absolute. The individual's ability to pay is important, regardless of the tax burden of other taxpayers. This is the material aspect of the hypothesis of incidence, chosen on the basis of tax equality, limiting the legislator's choice of tax base.

In a second step, the relative conception emerges, determining the amount of tax that is deemed to be consistent with tax equality. A comparative examination is made of the tax burden of one taxpayer in relation to the others, i.e. the amount of tax actually owed.

Objectively, the ability to pay corresponds to the wealth to be taxed, constituting the foundation or assumption of the tax, limiting the legislator in the choice of facts that constitute signs of wealth manifestation. Under the subjective or relative aspect, it would be the portion of this wealth that would be subject to taxation, observing individual conditions, i.e. it corresponds to what each person can effectively contribute to the general financing of the State.

2.2.2 The distinction is based on the taxable event of each tax

The doctrine links the rule of ability to pay, referring to the taxable event, objectively, disregarding comparative considerations. However, the principle of ability to pay, in relation to the tax base, is analyzed subjectively, in comparison with other taxpayers. This work diverges from these positions.

Since the ability to pay is a criterion of equality, it is the characteristic chosen by the constituent to be sought in the objects that must be compared in fiscal taxation. In other words, when taxation is aimed at funding the state machine, it is the ability to pay that will differentiate between taxpayers.

Some of the facts or situations chosen by the legislators to determine the size of the tax intensely demonstrate the characteristics of the people who will be in these situations and, in this case, will be facts that generate direct taxes. Other facts and situations chosen by legislators no longer have such a perceptible relationship with people, in which case they are indirect taxes. And we can't ignore the possibility of repercussions from the taxable person to third parties, which is more common in indirect taxes, but is also possible in some situations in direct taxes.

We therefore have the coexistence of personal taxes, whose triggering events are indicators of subjective contributory capacity, and non-personal taxes, whose triggering events are indicators of objective contributory capacity.

The subjectivity in question concerns that which is revealed when taxable events linked to personal circumstances occur, since the subjectivity of each taxable person, as proposed by most of the doctrine, is, in reality, unreachable. It should be noted, however, that the existential minimum and the prohibition of confiscation limit the application of the ability to pay taxes.

The criteria for a perfect distribution of the burden of maintaining the state will only be ideal when it is possible to identify the exact share of the individual's contribution in relation to the other individuals to the same extent. This level of transparency is only possible through a single tax. With the diversity of taxes, it is practically impossible to determine the appropriate tax for each individual.

The ability to pay, which is taken as the criterion of distinction, of equality, for defining the taxable event (rule) and the tax base (principle), is the one objectively indicated by consumption. Therefore, the tax must be returned to those who legally paid it. Although only the first agent in the chain bears the tax, everyone else is considered to be taxed. Therefore, anyone who fails to carry out the operation will be the holder of the credit against the state. Anyone who fails to carry out the presumed operation should be exempt.

2.3 Relationship between ability to pay and non-personal (indirect) taxes

2.3.1 The need for indirect taxes

Between 1918 and 1919, Johanes Popitz created business tax as a general consumption tax, on the occasion of the "Erzberger tax reform". This was a reaction to the realization of the principle of ability to pay on income tax, demanded by the states in Prussia, as BIRK (2006) reports.

In order to avoid a cumulative burden of taxation, value added tax was introduced in 1968. The criterion for this decision was the convenience of state taxation, a principle created by Adam Smith. Indirect taxation is, in general, unfair because it disregards the existential minimum and regressivity, according to BIRK (2006), as well as being less perceptible to citizens because they are embedded in the price of goods.

According to AVI-YONAH (2008), taxing consumption would be superior to taxing income, taking efficiency, fairness and practicality as criteria for evaluating fiscal policy.

2.3.2 Non-personal (indirect) taxes and their repercussions

Since the triggering event for indirect taxes is the event chosen as the sign of wealth that gives rise to the tax obligation, the ability to pay emerges objectively in this case. The repercussion, according to GIARDINA (1961), does not determine the transfer of the tax itself, or does so only minimally.

There is a concern to ensure that the tax on companies' sales is only levied on their profit, otherwise it will be levied on the assets that have already been overstated when the profit was made.

On the other hand, some can see the positives in the repercussion, given the high levels of income tax evasion. As TIPKE (2002) states, those who evade income tax will at least pay the tax passed on in the goods they consume. However, the author points out that, in fact, there will be double taxation on those who have not evaded income tax.

2.3.3 Theses against the applicability of the principle of ability to pay to indirect taxes

Doctrine differs on the application of the ability to pay to indirect taxation. PACHECO (2005), discussing the hypothesis of withholding from the source of payment of income tax, argues that the restricted contributory capacity is that of the legal recipient of the tax, and that, for the author, tax substitution is an accessory obligation, since the money collected is not their own, but that of the substitute. Thus, the emergence of the accessory obligation requires the prior emergence of the main obligation for the true taxpayer who bears the tax burden.

SCHIAVOLIN (1993) points out that taxes on industrialization and consumption are borne by consumers and, as a result, legislators are not required to be as closely linked to the ability to pay as in the case of direct taxes. His considerations are based on a circle he adopts to distinguish between de facto and de jure taxpayers, whereby the ability to pay would only have to be observed with regard to de jure taxpayers.

It is therefore important to conclude that the direct or indirect nature of taxation will be related to the subjective and objective aspects of both the rule and the principle of ability to pay.

2.3.4 Applicability of the ability-to-pay principle to indirect taxes

OLIVEIRA (1998) believes that the ability to pay applies to all taxes. LORENZON (1993) reserves the right to apply it to taxes that are not causally linked to any specific activity of the state. intended for the taxable person, in other words, to all taxes. NABAIS (2005) believes that income, assets and consumption are equivalent as indices of contributory capacity, establishing their application to indirect taxes. PALAO TABOADA (2005) points out that application should only take place in the fiscal function of the tax rule, concluding that it applies to both direct and indirect taxes.

In personal taxes, where the taxable event reveals personal circumstances, the rule requires that the hypothesis of incidence only and necessarily describes the manifestation of the ability to pay. The principle, in turn, must be optimized in order to define the circle of dimensioning of the fact that best resembles the real and specific event. In the case of non-personal taxes, the rule also requires that the hypothesis of incidence must be in line with the expression of the ability to pay and the principle also requires that the legislator, in defining the valuation criteria, seek to come as close as possible to the precise measurements of the real and specific event.

2.3.5 The rule of ability to pay is rarely applied to indirect and direct taxes

Due to the detailed nature of our constitutional system when it comes to tax powers, the ability-to-pay rule has a very restricted application. The hypotheses of incidence are all well defined, reducing the activity of the rule to a mere verification of the compatibility of the legislative product with the constitutional concept.

But not all facts are obvious expressions of wealth. The ICMS (tax on transactions involving the movement of goods), for example, depends on the meaning of the word "transactions". By choosing which behaviors fall under the jurisdiction of this exaggeration, we are defining which ones express the ability to pay. In this case, the ability to pay rule must be applied as a condition for the validity of these definitions.

2.4 Interventions to protect the principle of ability to pay in the name of practicability

As a principle, the ability to pay determines an ideal state to be pursued to the greatest extent possible, given the limitations that reality and the legal system impose on it. The existence of these limitations demonstrates the possibility of intervention in the fundamental right.

2.4.1 Hierarchical equality between all constitutional principles

As we have seen, simplification is one of the possible aims of tax rules. Aiming to apply tax rules to as many people as possible, their axiological nature emerges, insofar as they do not determine a course of action, but rather an ideal state of taxation to be optimized as far as possible. The same is true of the ability to pay. In this context, the structural distinction between principles and rules does not, and could not, establish any hierarchical degree between them. To conceive of the ability to pay in relation to the tax base as absolute would be to classify it as a rule, which is unacceptable, since no principle has an absolute nature, as TIPKE (1998) states.

2.4.2 Revisiting the functions of tax rules

Considering the complexity of the legal system, simplification is a necessity, even at the risk of interfering with fundamental rights. On the other hand, as TIPKE (2002) observes, practicability serves the principle of equality insofar as it reinforces generality, since practically unenforceable laws do not apply to everyone in the same way. Simplifying rules are based on the principle of practicability, which, by becoming a rule, is linked to equality.

2.4.3 Revisiting the cause of taxes

The rule, with its simplifying function, aims to maximize tax practicability, since the proportional application of the principles of structure in a relationship between ends and means.

Until the first theory of contributory capacity was formulated, the theory of equivalence prevailed, justifying the imposition of taxes on the basis of the taxpayer's participation in the general and particular advantages resulting from the activity and very existence of the state. The next step was to consider that the tax would be the citizens' contribution to the government for the achievement of collective ends without distinction, in other words, there would be a counter-payment by the state for collective services. The service would be the cause of the tax. Given the impossibility of measuring how much of this service was provided and how much was spent on each individual citizen, wealth was chosen as the criterion for distributing expenditure. Then came the ability to pay, expressing the possession or consumption of wealth as the cause, which emerges from the law, ultimately and immediately justifying the payment of taxes by the citizen.

The next phase was called the benefit theory, which linked the general provision of services by the state to taxation, without distinguishing between individual contributions. There was a gap in this model regarding those who were exempt from taxation due to their low ability to pay, insofar as they also benefited from indivisible state services.

The benefit theory made it possible to visualize the need for equivalence between a state's tax burden and what it converts into a benefit for society, leading to the sacrifice theory. According to the latter, the tax would be the cost of life in society and the state's renunciation of economic activity. Since one of the main aims of our Republic is to build a free, fair and solidary society, the participation of everyone in the costs of life in society expresses solidarity. The ability to pay therefore emerges as the foundation of taxation and as an expression of justice and solidarity.

In view of this, it is important to check which principle is being used to justify intervention in fundamental rights. Taxation is justified by the need to supply the state financially, with justice and solidarity. If there is no other extra-fiscal function, there is only the principle of funding the existence of the state, which does not carry out any economic activity. However, if the simplifying or inducing function is present, there is a possibility of intervention in the use of contributory capacity as a distinguishing criterion in the imposition of taxes. It is the fundamental right to pay a tax according to the wealth index objectively manifested by the fact that makes up the material aspect of the hypothesis of incidence, whether or not there are signs of personality.

CHAPTER 3
PROPORTIONALITY

3.1 Origins and theoretical evolution of the notion of proportionality

BONAVIDES (2008) states that there has been a rediscovery of the principle of proportionality over the last two hundred years in administrative law. From there it moved on to constitutional law with the crisis of positivism and the allocation of fundamental rights at the center of the legal order after the great wars, which led to the examination of proportionality being seen as a control of constitutionality in its own right. CRETTON (2001), in turn, reports that the origins of proportionality are confused with the origins of reasonableness, which would have occurred in 19th century France with the aim of restricting administrative power. It then evolved in Germany, in the 20th century, in the theory of fundamental rights, which was emphatically developed mainly in the post-war period. According to this author, in addition to the common origin, there is a very strong link between this principle and reasonableness.
REZEK NETO (2004) identifies four phases of the principle of proportionality in Brazilian law: as a legal principle in the strict sense, protecting citizens against abuses; as a legal principle in the context of the secondary system, as a norm limiting all state activity; as a general principle that binds all public agents; and, finally, as an implicit principle, as it is not expressly mentioned in the constitutional text.

BONAVIDES (2008) points out that the jurisprudence of the European courts uses this principle frequently and the doctrine defends its interpretation as a fundamental rule supporting fundamental rights, considering it an essential principle of the constitution.

However, there is a noticeable resistance in the doctrine to the application of proportionality beyond the limits of constitutional and administrative law, but BORGES (2004) warns that restrictions on fundamental rights can also be subject to judicial control in tax matters.

In Direct Unconstitutionality Action No. 551-1/RJ, which ruled that the fines imposed as minimums by the Rio de Janeiro State Constitution were unconstitutional, the confiscatory effect was argued, the boundaries of which were delimited based on the lack of reasonableness and proportionality of the penalties. It should be emphasized that the prohibition of confiscation in this judgment was placed as a rule, but confiscation is not prohibited to the maximum, but is allowed in certain situations, at least in tax matters, as long as it is based on constitutional grounds. Thus, the verification of the confiscatory effect would not be the most appropriate hypothesis for the application of proportionality.

Proportionality or reasonableness sometimes appears in case law in a material sense, as a parameter of justice. But more often than not, it appears as a tool for interpreting rules.

SILVA (2002) points out that the content of the proportionality rule goes beyond the prohibition of excess, and also means the prohibition of insufficiency.

3.1.1 The exclusion of proportionality from the class of principles

Proportionality, as conceptualized in this paper, is not identified as a proper content of principles because principles establish *prima facie* duties and not definitive duties. Therefore, its interpretation/application occurs through weighing and not subsumption and, if the formal instrument of that thought is proportionality, it cannot be confused with principles.

Proportionality is not characterized as the object of a formal principle because it does not have essential characteristics such as being realized in various degrees, the potential to clash with other principles and the direct prescription of ideal states of affairs rather than conduct. On the other hand, the admission of proportionality as a principle implies the hypothesis of its weighing up with other principles. Since it constitutes a method, its weighing would require the adoption of another method to do so. Since it is an instrument of dialogue between principles, it could not at the same time be the object of weighting.

Whether proportionality is simply applied or not raises the question of its normative nature.

3.2 Proportionality as a rule or as a normative application postulate

BONAVIDES (2008) describes proportionality as a criterion for limiting individual freedom. ALEXY (2008) classifies it as a formal rule because it is linked to the formal structure of weighing up principles. SILVA (2009) explains that, as a rule, proportionality prescribes a definitive duty. If it is to be applied, it is not subject to the factual and legal conditions of the specific case. It either applies in full or it doesn't.

Whether it is a postulate or a rule, proportionality cannot be seen as a principle, but as a prescription related to their application. It couldn't be a principle because that would confuse the rules to be applied and how this application would take place. Furthermore, the aim is to avoid talking about proportionality being weighted against other principles (as is the case with all principles) or even being restricted by such rules.

3.2.1 The legal-positive foundation

Authors often locate the legal basis for the notion of proportionality in equality, in due process of law (in its substantive dimension) and in the rule of law itself. Others locate it in Article 5 of the 1988 Constitution itself.

At this point, it is important to emphasize that positive law is not restricted to what is written down, but also includes the content of the meaning of the interpretation of texts and the countless relationships that these texts have with each other. The foundation (including validity) would lie in the structure of the legal norm, in the very structure of fundamental rights.

3.3 The three phases of applying proportionality

When faced with constitutional principles, be they fundamental rights or collective interests, they have to be harmonized with proportionality. In many cases, the proportional application of constitutional principles leads to intervention through a state measure which, on the other hand, is fulfilling the other principle involved in the issue.

It is therefore necessary for the principles to be applied proportionally, and not by subsumption, by analyzing the measure whose content is involved in terms of appropriateness, necessity and proportionality in the strict sense.

3.3.1 Suitability

Appropriateness, according to BONAVIDES (2008), is the pertinence between means and ends. The measure doesn't have to actually promote the desired end, it just has to be a potential means of achieving it. It is a measure of suitability for achieving the end.

SILVA (2002) highlights the sequential and subsidiary aspect in the analysis of the sub-rules of proportionality, since it only makes sense to analyze the necessity of a measure once it has been found to be appropriate, and the same goes for the examination of proportionality in the strict sense.

The suitability analysis must take into account the circumstances at the time of the analysis, with the information available at the time.

In addition, a principle depends on the appropriate means for its realization, and it is worth questioning whether there is a causal relationship between the measure questioned in relation to one principle and the realization of the other principle that collides with it.

3.3.2 The need

The examination of necessity must point to the absence of any other measure that would implement the principle in question with the same intensity, restricting the other conflicting principle to the minimum possible. The damage caused by the state measure that intervenes in fundamental rights must be limited to what is essential.

The sense of necessity that is being asserted does not have an imposing character. It is better described as an examination of comparisons between alternative measures, choosing the one that imposes the least restriction on the fundamental right that is the object of the intervention. If the alternative measures present the same level of restriction, the levels of adequacy must be examined. If both are equally suitable, the one that imposes the least restriction is chosen.

Finally, it is important to note that the definitive decision in the examination of necessity is the one that examines the effectiveness of the measure.

We will then move on to analyze the legal limitations on the effectiveness of the principles, translated into proportionality in the strict sense.

3.3.3 Proportionality in the strict sense

This examination assesses the intensity of the realization of one principle and the importance of the realization of the other principle. The question is whether, in specific circumstances, the positive effects of a higher density principle outweigh the negative effects of the lower density legal principle. The non-fulfillment of the other principle is not necessary for the measure to fail the proportionality test in the strict sense, nor is it necessary for the essential core of a fundamental right to be affected. It is enough that the reasons behind the intervention are not strong enough to justify the deleterious effects on the fundamental right affected.

According to ALEXY (2008), the analysis should start with the degree of intervention in one right, followed by an examination of the importance of the other principle, so that the gain (or not) brought about by the restriction can be compared and the measure considered justified or not.

CHAPTER 4

THE INTERVENTION IN THE PRINCIPLE OF CONTRIBUTORY CAPACITY AUTHORIZED BY ART. 150, §7, OF THE 1988 CONSTITUTION

4.1 The content of the constitutional provision and the legal rules on taxation by presumed taxable event

4.1.1 The constitutional rule of jurisdiction

The rule introduced by Constitutional Amendment No. 3/93 empowers political entities to establish the forward tax substitution system by law. As a rule of competence, it must be systematically harmonized with the other constitutional rules limiting the power to tax. Although it grants the power to tax, it is undoubtedly a limiting rule because it conditions its use in various respects, such as the immediate and preferential return of amounts in the event of the presumed taxable event not occurring.

Art. 150, §7 of the Constitution provides an exception to Art. 145, §1 of the same law, to which two commands can be attributed: a rule regarding the triggering events of taxes and related contributions and a principle regarding the basis for calculating these taxes.

The exercise of this exceptional power by legislators, however, does not escape the general rules concerning tax legislation, especially with regard to the definition of taxes and their types, as well as, with regard to itemized taxes, the definition of the triggering events, calculation basis and taxpayers; tax obligation, payment, credit, prescription and decay of taxes; adequate tax treatment of the cooperative act practiced by cooperatives (art. 146, III, a, b and c of the Constitution).

However, as this is an exception rule, it must be interpreted restrictively. In addition, there is a need to seek the end sought by the rule, which highlights the importance of analyzing the cause of taxes, as their justification and scope.

The ability to pay is the very cause of the taxes and contributions that are identified with it, as something that justifies and gives meaning to the rule, which denotes the exceptional nature of the competence brought by art. 150, §7, of the Constitution.

To claim that the derived constituent made a weighting and privileged, through a rule, practicability to the detriment of the guarantee of taxation in accordance with the ability to pay, would be to leave it to the legislator to unravel the entire constitutional order, violating Art. 3, I, of the Constitution. This would lead to the unconstitutionality of Amendment No. 3/93, as it violates the petrea clause which states that the objective of our Republic is to build a free, just and solidary society.

4.1.2 The legal rules of taxation by presumed taxable event

The original wording of the National Tax Code provided for forward tax substitution, in Article 58, §2, II, through which the legislator could assign responsibility to the manufacturer or wholesaler. On 01/30/1967, Complementary Act No. 34 changed the wording of the provision, which was changed again on 12/31/1968 by Decree-Law No. 406, which replaced the entire chapter of the CTN dealing with ICM, while maintaining its essence. On December 7, 1983, a new amendment was made by Complementary Law No. 44.

Since the 1988 Constitution, the member states, based on art. 34, §8, of the Transitional Constitutional Provisions Act, have provisionally regulated tax substitution through ICM Convention No. 66/88. This convention was replaced by Complementary Law 87/96, given the need for a complementary law to regulate tax substitution.

The use of the expression "forward tax substitution by presumed taxable event" raises some unnecessary difficulties in interpretation, such as, for example, that it would be a tax obligation without a taxable event or that the tax relationship arises before the taxable event occurs. Doctrine is also divided on whether this system uses presumptions or fictions.

Following the reasoning of the Supreme Court's decision in ADI No. 1851-4/AL, the taxable event is definitive. And, since this judgment is the methodological premise of this work, it is possible to equate the issue more simply.

The presumption always relates to the past, not the future. There is no doctrine, either in procedural law or in procedural tax law, in which the presumption appears as proof of a future fact.

The legal treatment given to presumptions in our tax law is out of the ordinary, not to mention the obvious contradiction in collecting the tax in advance without the prior or concomitant occurrence of its taxable event.

Article 114 of the National Tax Code states that the taxable event is the situation defined by law as necessary and sufficient for its occurrence. And art. 113, §1 of the same law states that the main obligation arises with the occurrence of the taxable event. Therefore, when the law establishes that the first operation in the commercial cycle of a good gives rise to the obligation to pay tax, there is no need to speak of a presumption, but of a taxable event.

Nor is it a fiction, because there is no equating of hypotheses with the same consequence. There is no way to equate the first sale of a cycle with the next sale or even with the final sale. They are different calculation bases. It is not possible to equate the tax base of the initial sale with the tax base of the sale to the final consumer before it takes place.

In the so-called "forward tax substitution by presumed taxable event", the tax is levied on consumption, at the beginning of the commercial cycle. The tax obligation arises with the taxable event defined by law and is extinguished with the payment of the tax, subject to the occurrence of subsequent operations.

Under this system, the basis for calculating this tax obligation is an estimate of the monetary expression of the consumption on which it falls, which violates the guarantee of taxation according to the ability to pay, which is authorized by the Constitution, provided that it respects the limits of appropriateness, necessity and proportionality in the strict sense.

4.2 The appropriateness of presumed taxable event taxation

Since taxes aim to fund the state in solidarity, according to the ability to pay, the latter should be the criterion to be observed.

If there is an extrafiscal nature to the exaggeration, it is possible to distance oneself from this criterion, as long as the measure is suitable for promoting this other function.

The practicability of taxation can also justify departing from the ability-to-pay criterion in order to achieve the ideal state of affairs by simplifying tax rules.

However, collection as a justification for making the guarantee of the ability to pay more flexible cannot be seen generically, lest it become an instrument for arbitrarily increasing revenue through estimated calculation bases that are higher than reality.

4.2.1 The confusion between practicability and fundamental rights

While practicability may violate the ability to pay, it contributes to it by distributing the tax burden under the collective vision of the ability to pay. The collective interest, in this case, is that all facts that fall within the hypothesis of incidence described in the rule should be taxed.

But it is important to emphasize that tax collection and its practicability have nothing to do with fundamental rights. The duty to pay taxes is a legal duty, and the adjective fundamental does not seem sufficient to equate them in any way with fundamental rights.

Classically, fundamental rights are individual rights against state power. Social rights are rights to a state service, as long as they are constitutionally provided for. If there is no provision allowing a taxpayer to demand taxation from someone else, they cannot be equated with fundamental rights.

Furthermore, equating fundamental rights with such duties has no effect. It is unimaginable that the duty to tax should be maximized in order to generate the duty to pay as much tax as possible, unless there is a demonstration of factual or legal impossibility.

Finally, taxation is already, in itself, the result of the weighting, drawn up by the constituent assembly, between the collective interest of building a free, fair and solidary society and the rights of freedom and property. From this weighting, rules of jurisdiction were established, and there are no other principles capable of justifying the extension of these rules.

4.2.2 The levels of abstraction, generality and timeliness of the adequacy

According to AVILA (2008), measures to intervene in the ability to pay, with taxation based on a presumed taxable event, do not need to be concretely appropriate in order to actually produce the favorable effects that justify it, it is enough that they have the potential to produce such an effect.

As for generality, the aforementioned author states that the presumed taxable event system should be suitable for the majority of cases, without the need to investigate each individual case.

Adequacy, in turn, must take into account the time when it was adopted, avoiding the possibility of "supervening inadequacy".

AVILA's (2008) doctrine is intrinsically related to the capture of contributory capacity by the average. If there are unequal effects of a reasonably extensive and continuous nature, the standard is not reflecting the average. Considering that standardization is an instrument for balancing equality itself, there is no denying the coherence of this author's reasoning.

Thus, it is not a question of the actual price in each specific case. The calculation base is formed by applying standardized value-added margins for each type of business or commodity. Therefore, those who sell above the average are subject to a lower real rate than the nominal one, and vice versa, which is not prohibited by our legal system as long as this margin does not deviate from the average reality.

In addition, this margin must be established on the basis of a proper survey of prices, drawn up under due legal process, since the taxpayer has no way of checking whether the standard adopted actually corresponds to reality.

Another point is that setting up this tax substitution system in productive sectors with a large number of agents has a strong tendency to be inappropriate in terms of practicality, leading to disproportionality and unconstitutionality, since one of the great advantages of this system is to concentrate main and ancillary obligations on a small number of taxpayers, as happens in the alcoholic beverages sector, for example. If it doesn't even have the potential to reduce the number of taxpayers, the inadequacy is obvious. The same applies if there is no branch at the end of the production chain.

4.3 The need for presumed taxable event taxation

A measure is considered necessary if, among other available and equally appropriate measures, it imposes the least restriction on the fundamental right to taxation according to ability to pay.

The first measure with effects very close to the regime studied is the increase in the tax base of the taxpayer located at the beginning of the commercial cycle, exempting the other agents in the same cycle. This measure has the advantage of avoiding talk of payment by the taxpayer or by the substitute, and also diverts discussion away from the presumed taxable event.

However, it is undeniable that this measure imposes greater restrictions as it does not guarantee the return of the values corresponding to a stage of the cycle that does not occur.

The possible alternative is to increase the tax rate, exempting the following operations. This model also fails to solve the problem of the missed stage, while making it difficult to calculate the amounts corresponding to that operation.

With this, we can see that the alternatives that seem to bring the same adequacy, in fact, imply a greater restriction on the ability to pay. Therefore, in the abstract, the measure is necessary.

4.4 The proportionality in the strict sense of presumed taxable event taxation

The rules on taxation by presumed taxable event restrict the guarantee of taxation according to the ability to pay, and the constitutional limits of this intervention remain to be defined.

As we have seen, this is an abstractly adequate and necessary system, provided that there is not too much discrepancy in relation to the average values practiced, nor in relation to the number of taxpayers who must necessarily be reduced by adopting this taxation technique.

Under the prism of proportionality in the strict sense, the gain in practicability and generality of the application of the tax law that justifies the restriction on the fundamental right of ability to pay must be assessed.

The search for the effective contributory capacity of each taxpayer leads to the complexity of defining the tax base, causing legal uncertainty.

The principle of practicability must be applied in harmony with the other principles, so that its presumptions and generalizations effectively correspond to the average of normality, admitting and facilitating counter-evidence so that justice can be done in extreme individual cases.

In view of this, GARCIA NOVOA (2006) defends the adoption of the objective assessment of taxes as a definition of alternative methods of measuring the tax base. Objective systems will only violate the ability to pay when they distance themselves from the tax base and cease to be an instrument for measuring it. It is therefore possible to partially renounce individual justice in order to avoid the general injustice resulting from evasion. Any unconstitutionality stems from its disproportionality.

But, as you can see, in general, the appropriateness and necessity of these rules can be seen, and they will need to be assessed in terms of their practicality, which translates into proportionality in the strict sense.

CONCLUSION

At the same time as it expresses a principle, such as a *prima facie* duty, the ability to pay is also seen as a definitive duty, typical of legal rules. As a rule, the ability to pay requires the legislator to choose as taxable events only events that express wealth that can be taxed. As a principle, the definition of the tax base must obey quantification criteria that seek the maximum individualization of the specific taxable event.

In personal taxes, the ability to pay will be expressed subjectively and, in events that express wealth without personal references, ability will be analyzed objectively in order to maintain it as a criterion of equality.

In its axiological sense, the ability to pay has its application limited to the specific factual and legal possibilities of the specific case. Its restriction, however, is limited to factual and legal justifications consisting of other constitutional principles, which may be collective interests, as is usually the case in tax matters. In this paper, we aim to analyze the hypothesis in the light of the collective interest in the practicability of taxation.

The practicability measure studied was the system of forward tax substitution by presumed taxable event, authorized by a constitutional rule that must be interpreted within the strict limits of proportionality, that is, in view of the criteria of appropriateness, necessity and proportionality in the strict sense.

If the measure is causally related to the intended purpose, it is appropriate. Among the appropriate measures, the one that imposes the least restriction on the guarantee of the ability to pay will be considered necessary. Strictly speaking, proportionality means, in each case, that which promotes gains in favor of the principle that justify the loss to the detriment of the other.

In this sense, it is important to emphasize that both the rule in art. 150, §7, of the Constitution, and

Complementary Law 87/96, are already the result of considerations between the ability to pay and practicality, on the part of the derived constituent and the national legislator. However, we are not saying that this necessarily means that all the rules on taxation by presumed taxable event are appropriate and necessary, as there may be cases in which the system proves to be inappropriate or unnecessary.

In view of the appropriateness and necessity, it is a question of assessing the criterion of proportionality in the strict sense of the measure, in order to verify whether, in that particular economic sector, there will in fact be a gain in practicability that justifies sacrificing the guarantee of taxation according to the ability to pay.

BIBLIOGRAPHICAL REFERENCES:

ALEXY, Robert. ***Theory of fundamental rights***. Spanish translation by Ernesto Garzon Valdez. Madrid: *Centro de Estudios Politicosy Constitucionales:* 2001.

. **Theory of fundamental rights**. Brazilian translation by Virgilio Afonso da Silva. Sao Paulo: Malheiros, 2008.

ATALIBA, Geraldo. **Hipotese de incidencia tributaria**. 6. ed. Sao Paulo: Malheiros, 2008.

; BARRETO, Aires Fernandino. Substituigao e responsabilidade tributaria. In **Revista de Direito Tributario**, Sao Paulo, ano 13, n. 49, p. 73-99, jul./set. 1989.

AVILA, Humberto. ICMS. Tax Substitution in the State of São Paulo. Calculation basis. Tax Tariff. State Legislative Competence to return the Constant Difference between the Price Usually Practiced and the Price in the Tariff. Examination of Constitutionality. **Revista Dialetica de Direito Tributario**, Sao Paulo, n. 124, p. 92- 111, Jan. 2006.

. Tax on the Circulation of Goods - ICMS. Tax Substitution. Calculation Basis. Tax Tariff. Maximum Consumer Price. Constant Difference between the Price Usually Practiced and the Price in the Tariff or the Maximum Consumer Price Suggested by the Manufacturer. Examination of Constitutionality. **Revista Dialetica de Direito Tributario**, Sao Paulo, n. 123, p. 122-134, Dec. 2005.

. Presumptions and tax guidelines in the face of administrative efficiency. In: ROCHA, Valdir de Oliveira (Coord.). **Grandes questões atuais do direito tributario.** Sao Paulo: Dialetica, 2005. v. 9, p. 277-288.

. Proportionality and tax law. In: Luis Eduardo Schoueri (coord.), **Direito Tributario: homenagem a Alcides Jorge Costa**, V. I, (329-347). Sao Paulo: Quartier Latin, 2003, p. 329-347.

. **Sistema constitucional tributario: de acordo com emenda constitucional n. 42**, de 19.12.03.

Sao Paulo: Saraiva, 2004.

. **Theory of Tax Equality**. Sao Paulo: Malheiros, 2008.

Theory of principles: from the definition to the application of legal principles. 8. ed. Sao Paulo: Malheiros, 2008.

AVI-YONAH, Reuven S. The three objectives of taxation. Translated by Luis Flavio Neto, In: **Revista direito tributario atual**, v. 22 (7-29). Sao Paulo: IBDT/Dialetica, 2008, p.7-29.

AYALA, Jose Luis Perez de. ***Explication de la tecnica de los impuestos*** . 3. ed. Madrid: *Editorales de Derecho Reunidas,* 1981.

BALEEIRO, Aliomar. **Brazilian tax law**. 11. ed. updated by Misabel Abreu Machado Derzi. Rio de Janeiro: Forense, 2007.

. **Constitutional Limitations on the Power to Tax . 7. ed. rev. e compl. a luz da Constituigao de 1988 até a Emenda Constitucional n° 10/1996**. updated by Misabel Abreu Machado Derzi. Rio de Janeiro: Forense, 1997.

BANDEIRA DE MELLO, Celso Antonio. **Course in administrative law**. Sao Paulo: 2007.

BARRETO, Aires Fernandino. **Base de calculo, aliquota e princípios constitucionais** . 2. ed. Sao Paulo: Max Limonad, 1998.

; GIARDINO, Cleber. Presumptions in tax law. In: MARTINS, Ives Gandra da Silva (Coord.) **Caderno de pesquisas tributarias** . Sao Paulo: Resenha Tributaria, 1984. v. 9, p. 185-250.

BASTO, 1o8ë Guilherme Xavier de. **Consumption taxation and its international coordination**. Lisbon: Center for Fiscal Studies, 1991 (Cadernos de Ciencia e Tecnica Fiscal).

BECHO, Renato Lopes. **Tax liability**. Sao Paulo: Diactica, 2000.

BECKER, Alfredo Augusto. **General theory of tax law**. 4 ed. Sao Paulo: Noeses, 2007.

BIRK, Dieter. ***Diritto tributario tedesco***. Italian translation by Enrico de Mita. Milan: Giuffre Editore, 2006.

BONAVIDES, Paulo. **Constitutional Law Course**. Sao Paulo: Malheiros, 2008.

BORGES, сзё Souto Maior. Social Contributions (PIS/COFINS) and the Jurisprudence of the STF. In **Revista Dialetica**, Sao Paulo, n. 118, p. 76-91, jul. 2005.

BRASIL. Codigo tributario nacional. 18. ed. Sao Paulo: Saraiva, 2012.

. National Finance Policy Council. Convenio ICMS n° 66, Brasilia, March 29, 1988. Extends the deadline for granting the tax incentive provided for in Convenio ICM 28/81, of December 17, 1981. DOU, Brasilia, March 31. 1988. Available at: <http://www.fazenda.gov.b r/confaz/>. Accessed on: September 6, 2013.

. National Finance Policy Council. ICMS Convention No. 13, Florianopolis, March 21, 1997. Harmonizes procedure regarding the application of § 7, article 150, of the Federal Constitution and article 10 of Complementary Law 87/96, of 13.09.96. DOU, Brasilia, March 25. 1997a. Available at: <http://www.fazenda.gov.br/confaz/>. Accessed on: September 6, 2013.

. National Finance Policy Council. ICMS Convention No. 70, Manaus, July 25, 1997. Provides for the value-added margin in setting the ICMS calculation basis for the purpose of determining the tax due by tax substitution in subsequent operations. DOU, Brasilia, August 5, 1997b. Available at: <http://www.fazenda.gov.br/confaz/>. Accessed on: September 15, 2013.

. Constitution (1988). Constitution of the Federative Republic of Brazil, of October 5, 1988. DOU, Brasilia, October 6, 1988. Available at:<http://www.planalto.gov.br/ccivil_03/Constituicao/Constituicao.htm>. Accessed on:

September 6, 2013.

. Complementary Law No. 44, of December 7, 1983. Amends Decree-Law No. 406, of December 31, 1968, which establishes general tax law rules, and makes other provisions. DOU, Brasilia, December 8, 1983. Available at:<http://www.planalto.gov.br/ccivil_03/Leis/LCP/Lcp44.htm>. Accessed on: September 6, 2013.

. Complementary Law No. 5.172, of October 25, 1966. Provides for the National Tax System and establishes general tax law rules applicable to the Union, States and Municipalities. DOU, Brasilia, October 27, 1966. Available at: <http://www.planalto.gov.br/ccivil_03/Leis/L5172.htm>. Accessed on: September 6, 2013.

. Complementary Law No. 7, of September 7, 1970. Establishes the Social Integration Program, and makes other provisions. DOU, Brasilia, September 8, 1970. Available at: <http://www.planalto.gov.br/ccivil_03/Leis/LCP/Lcp07.htm>. Accessed on: September 6, 2013.

. Complementary Law No. 70, of December 30, 1991. Institutes contribution to financing of Social Security, raises the rate of the social contribution on the profits of financial institutions and makes other provisions. DOU, Brasilia, Dec. 31, 1991. Available at: <http://www.planalto.gov.br/ccivil_03/Leis/LCP/Lcp70.htm>. Accessed on: September 6, 2010.

. Complementary Law No. 87, of September 13, 1996. Provides for state and Federal District taxes on operations relating to the circulation of goods and on the provision of interstate and intercity transportation and communication services, and makes other provisions. (Kandir Law). DOU, Brasilia, September 16, 1996. Available <http://www.planalto.gov.br/ccivil_03/Leis/LCP/Lcp87.htm>. Accessed on: September 6, 2013.

. Law No. 10.406, of January 10, 2002. Establishes the Civil Code. DOU, Brasilia, January 11, 2002. Available at: <http://www.planalto.gov.br/ccivil_03/leis/2002/L10406.htm>. Accessed on: September 24, 2013.

. Superior Court of Justice. REsp n° 203.551/MG. 2. T. Rel. Min. Ari Pargendler, j. 18/03/1999. DJ , Brasilia, 03 May 1999. p. 138. Available at:<http://www.stj.jus.br>.Accessed on: 26 Sept. 2013.

. Superior Court of Justice. REsp n° 265.343/SP. 1. T. Rel. Min. Garcia Vieira, Rel. p/ Acordao Ministro Humberto Gomes de Barros, j. 21/11/2000. DJ, Brasilia, June 11, 2001. p. 115. Available at: <http://www.stj.jus.br>. Accessed on: September 26, 2013.

. Superior Court of Justice. RMS No. 13.294/MA. 2. T. Rel. Min. Paulo Medina, j. 04/06/2002. DJ , Brasilia, Dec. 19, 2002. p. 352. Available at: <http://www.stj.jus.br>. Accessed on: September 15, 2013.

. Superior Court of Justice. RMS No. 18.473/PA. 1. T. Rel. Min. Francisco Falcao, j. 08/11/2005. DJ, Brasilia, Dec. 19, 2005. p. 209. Available at:<http://www.stj.jus.br>. Accessed on: September 15, 2013.

. Superior Court of Justice. RMS No. 18.677/MT. 2. T. Rel. Min. Castro Meira, j. 19/04/2005. DJ, Brasilia, June 20, 2005. p. 175. Available at: <http://www.stj.jus.br>. Accessed on: September 15, 2013.

. Superior Court of Justice. RMS No. 19.080/MT. 1. T. Rel. Min. Francisco Falcao, j. 18/10/2005. DJ, Brasilia, Dec. 19, 2005. p. 210. Available at: <http://www.stj.jus.br>. Accessed on: September 15, 2013.

. Superior Court of Justice. REsp n° 740.900/RS. 2. T. Rel. Minister Eliana Calmon, j. 19/10/2006. DJ, Brasilia, 31 Oct. 2006. p. 263. Available at: <http://www.stj.gov.br>.Accessed on: 15 Sep. 2013.

. Superior Court of Justice. EDcl no REsp n° 374.449/MG. 2. T. Rel. Min. Joao Otavio de Noronha, j. 23/10/2007. DJ, Brasilia, 22 Nov. 2007. p. 224. Available at:

<http://www.stj.jus.br>. Accessed on: September 26, 2013.

. Superior Court of Justice. AgRg no Ag n° 903.224/MG. 2. T. Rel. Min. Eliana Calmon, j. 11/12/2007. DJ, Brasilia, 07 feb. 2008a. p. 307. Available at: <http://www.stj.jus.br>. Accessed on: September 26, 2013.

. Superior Court of Justice. REsp n° 919.363/DF. 1. T. Rel. Min. Luiz Fux, j. 19/06/2008. DJ, Brasilia, 07 Aug. 2008b. Available at: <http://www.stj.jus.br>. Accessed on: September 26, 2013.

. Superior Court of Justice. AgRg no Ag n° 985.009/MG. 2. T. Rel. Min. Castro Meira, j. 19/08/2008. DJe, Brasilia, September 11, 2008c. Available at:<http://www.stj.jus.br>. Accessed on: September 26, 2010.

. Superior Court of Justice. AgRg no REsp n° 809.752/RJ. 2. T. Rel. Min. Mauro Campbell Marques, j. 04/09/2008. DJe , Brasilia, 06 Oct. 2008d. Available at: <http://www.stj.jus.br>. Accessed on: September 26, 2013.

. Superior Court of Justice. RMS No. 22.136/RJ. 1. T. Rel. Min. Luiz Fux, j. 21/10/2008. DJe , Brasilia, 13 nov. 2008e. Available at: <http://www.stj.jus.br>. Accessed on: September 26, 2013.

. Superior Court of Justice. REsp n° 952.883/RJ. 2. T. Rel. Minister Eliana Calmon, j. 17/03/2009. DJe , Brasilia, May 25, 2009a. Available at: <http://www.stj.jus.br>. Accessed on: September 15, 2013.

. Superior Court of Justice. REsp n° 1.111.156/SP. 1. T. Rel. Min. Humberto Martins, j. 14/10/2009. DJe, Brasilia, October 22, 2009. Available at: <http://www.stj.jus.br>. Accessed on: September 26, 2013.

. Superior Court of Justice. RMS No. 24.374/MG. 2.T. Rel. Min. Castro Meira, j. 18/02/2010. DJe , Brasilia, Feb. 26, 2010. Available at:<http://www.stj.jus.br>. Accessed on: September 26, 2013.

. Superior Court of Justice. REsp n° 1.176.356/RJ. 2. T. Rel. Min. Herman Benjamin, j. 16/03/2010. DJe, Brasilia, March 26, 2010. Available at: <http://www.stj.jus.br>. Accessed on: September 26, 2013.

. Superior Court of Justice. REsp n° 1.166.177/AM. 1. T. Rel. Min. Hamilton Carvalhido, j. 28/05/2010. DJe , Brasilia, June 2, 2010c. Available at: <http://www.stj.jus.br>. Accessed on: September 26, 2013.

. Superior Court of Justice. EDcl no AgRg no REsp n° 1.175.879/RJ. 2. T. Rel. Min. Humberto Martins, j. 15/06/2010. DJe, Brasilia, June 22, 2010d. Available at: <http://www.stj.jus.br>. Accessed on: September 26, 2013.

. Superior Court of Justice. AgRg nos EDcl no REsp n° 760.494/RJ. 2. T. Rel. Min. Castro Meira, j. 15/06/2010.DJe , Brasilia, 28 jun. 2010e. Available at: <http://www.stjjus.br>. Accessed on: September 26, 2013.

. Superior Court of Justice. AgRg no Ag n° 1.221.742/SP. 1. T. Rel. Min. Luiz Fux, j. 15/06/2010. DJe, Brasilia, June 30, 2010f. Available at: <http://www.stj.jus.br>. Accessed on: September 26, 2013.

. Superior Court of Justice. REsp n° 1.192.409/SE. 2. T. Rel. Minister Eliana Calmon, j. 22/06/2010. DJe , Brasilia, 01 jul. 2010g. Available at: <http://www.stj.jus.br>. Accessed on: September 15, 2013.

. Superior Court of Justice. REsp n° 1.098.304/MG. 2. T. Rel. Ministra Eliana Calmon,j. 05/08/2010.DJe, Brasilia, 17 aug.2010h. Available at: <http://www.stj.jus.br>. Accessed on: September 26, 2013.

. Superior Court of Justice. REsp n° 1.160.253/MG. 2. T. Rel. Min. Castro Meira, j. 10/08/2010. DJe, Brasilia, August 19, 2010i. Available at:<http://www.stj.jus.br>. Accessed on: September 26, 2013.

. Superior Court of Justice. Sumula n° 166.DJU, Brasilia, 27 aug. 1996. p. 2.996. Available at: <http://www.stj.jus.br>. Accessed on: September 26, 2013.

. Superior Court of Justice. Sumula n° 375.DJe , Brasilia, 30 mar. 2009. Available at: <http://www.stj.jus.br>. Accessed on: September 26, 2013.

. Superior Court of Justice. Sumula n° 431. DJe, Brasilia, May 13, 2010. Available at: <http://www.stj.jus.br>. Accessed on: September 26, 2013.

. Federal Supreme Court. AI n° 131.941-1. Rel. Min. Marco Aurelio, j. 09/04/1991. DJ , Brasilia, 19 abr. 1991. p. 4.583. Available at: <http://www.stf.jus.br>. Accessed on: September 26, 2013.

. Federal Supreme Court. RE n° 116.121/SP. Rel. Min. Marco Aurelio, j. 11/10/2000. DJ , Brasilia, May 25, 2001. p. 17. Available at: <http://www.stf.jus.br>.Accessed on: Sept. 26. 2013.

. Federal Supreme Court. AI n° 460.422 AgR. Rel. Min. Celso de Mello, j. 08/06/2004. DJ, Brasília, June 25, 2004. p. 42. Available at: <http://www.stf.jus.br>. Accessed on: September 26, 2013.

. Federal Supreme Court. RE n° 401.552 AgR. Rel. Min. Eros Grau, j. 21/09/2004. DJ, Brasília, October 15, 2004. p. 12. Available at: <http://www.stf.jus.br>. Accessed on: September 26, 2013.

. Federal Supreme Court. RE n° 390.840-5/MG. Rel. Min. Marco Aurelio, j. 09/11/2005. DJ, Brasília, August 15, 2005. p. 25. Available at: <http://www.stf.jus.br>. Accessed on: September 26, 2013.

. Federal Supreme Court. RE n° 255.682 AgR. Rel. Min. Carlos Velloso, j. 29/11/2005. DJ, Brasília, Feb. 10, 2006. Available at: <http://www.stf.jus.br>. Accessed on: September 26, 2013.

. Federal Supreme Court. AI n° AI-AgR 682.680/RJ. Rel. Min. Eros Grau, j. 20/05/2008.DJ, Brasília, 06 jun. 2008. Available at: <http://www.stf.jus.br>. Accessed on: September 26, 2013.

. Federal Supreme Court. Sumula Vinculante n° 31. DJU, Brasília, March 5, 2010. Available at: <http://www.stj.jus.br>. Accessed on: September 26, 2013.

CANTO, Gilberto de Ulhoa. Presumptions in tax law. In: MARTINS, Ives Gandra da Silva (Coord.) **Caderno de pesquisas tributarias.** Sao Paulo: Resenha Tributaria, 1984. v. 9, p. 1-33.

CARRAZZA, Roque Antonio. **Course in constitutional tax law**. 3. ed. rev. ampl. e atual. pela Constituigao Federal de 1988. Sao Paulo: Revista dos Tribunais, 1991.

. ICMS . 10 ed. Sao Paulo: Malheiros, 2005. CARVALHO, Paulo de Barros. **Tax law course**. 4. ed. Sao Paulo: Saraiva, 1991.

. Teoria da norma tributaria. Sao Paulo: Lael, 1974. CASTRO, Carlos Alberto Farracha de. Preservation of the company in the civil code.Curitiba: Jurua, 2007.

CARVALHO, Paulo de Barros. Constitutional tax principles in the Brazilian positive system. In: Ives Gandra da Silva Martins e Andre Elali (coord.), **Elementos actuais de direito tributario.** (391/416). Curitiba: Jurua, 2005, pp. 391/416.

COELHO, Sacha Calmon Navarro. Progressive tax substitution and the charging of ICMS on any increase in fuel volume due to variations in ambient temperature. In: COELHO, Sacha Calmon Navarro. **Tax law: current issues.** Sao Paulo: Quartier Latin, 2006a. p. 347-369.

. **Comentarios a constituigao de 1988: sistema tributario**. Rio de Janeiro: Forense, 2005.

. Contributions in Brazilian law - their problems and solutions. In: COELHO, Sacha Calmon Navarro (Coord).**Contributes para a seguridade social** . Sao Paulo: Quartier Latin, 2007a. p. 17-63.

. **Curso de direito tributario brasileiro**.9. ed. Rio de Janeiro: Forense,2007b.

. Legal certainty and legal changes. In: ROCHA, Valdir de Oliveira (Coord.). **Grandes questões**

atuais do direito tributario. Sao Paulo: Dialdtica, 2006b. v. 10, p. 402-431.

. Direct and indirect liability - tax substitution. In: ROCHA, Valdir de Oliveira (Coord.). **Grandes questões atuais do direito tributario.** Sao Paulo: Dialdtica, 2009. v.13, p. 357-382.

. **Teoria geral do tributo e da exoneração tributaria**. 3. ed. Belo Horizonte: Del Rey, 1999.

; DERZI, Misabel Abreu Machado. ICMS tax substitution and the protection of trust. In : COELHO, Sacha Calmon Navarro. **Tax law: current issues**. Sao Paulo: Quartier Latin, 2006. p. 371-430.

COSTA, Alcides Jorge. Contributory capacity. In **Revista de Direito Tributario**, v. 55 (297302). Sao Paulo: Jan-Mar. 1991, pp. 297-302.

COSTA, Regina Helena. **Principle of contributory capacity**. Sao Paulo: Malheiros, 2003.

CRETTON, Ricardo Aziz. **The principles of proportionality and reasonableness and their application in tax law**. Rio de Janeiro: Lumen Juris, 2001.

DERZI, Misabel Abreu Machado**. The unpredictability of case law and the effects of Supreme Court decisions on tax law**. Belo Horizonte, 2007a. (Unpublished).

. **Direito tributario, direito penal e tipo** . 2. ed. rev. e atual. Sao Paulo: Revista dos Tribunais, 2007b.

. Distortions of the principle of non-cumulative taxation in the ICMS: comparison with European VAT. In: COELHO, Sacha Calmon Navarro. **Temas de direito tributario**.Belo Horizonte: Del Rey, 1988. p. 107-151.

. **Changes in case law: protection of trust, objective good faith and non-retroactivity as constitutional limitations on the power to tax**. Sao Paulo: Noeses, 2009.

. The principle of corporate preservation and the right to tax savings. In: ROCHA, Valdir de Oliveira (Coord.).**Grandes questões actuais do direito tributario.** Sao Paulo: Dialdtica, 2006. v. 10, p. 336-358.

. Practicality. ICMS. Progressive, "forward" substitution. In: DERZI,Misabel Abreu Machado (Coord.).**Construindo o direito tributario na constituigao: uma analise da obra do Ministro Carlos Mario Velloso**. Belo Horizonte:Del Rey, 2004. p. 167-190.

. Breaches of free competition in ICMS, IPI and PIS-COFINS: corporatism, informality, broad residual cumulativeness and tax substitution. **Revista Internacional de Direito Tributario**, Belo Horizonte, n. 3, p. 103-117, jan./jun. 2005.

. On the lack of respect for the constitutional principles of non-cumulative nature (neutrality), selectivity and ability to pay in consumption taxes. **Revista da Associagao Brasileira de Direito Tributario**, Belo Horizonte, ano III, n. 5/6, p. 181-197, jan./ago. 2000.

DWORKIN, Ronald. ***Taking rights seriously***. Cambridge (Massachusetts): Harvard University Press, 1977.

ETCHEGOYEN, Marcos F. Garcia.***El principio de capacidad contributiva.Evolucion dogmatica y preyeccion en el derecho argentino*** *.Buenos* Aires: Editoa Abaco de Rodolfo Depalma, 2004.

FERRAZ, Roberto. Consumption, competition, the market and the distortions of tax substitution (forward). In: ROCHA, Valdir de Oliveira (Coord.). **Grandes questões atuais do direito tributario.** Sao Paulo: Dialdtica, 2007. v. 11, p. 359-379.

GARCIA NOVOA, Cesar. *The challenge of simplifying tax systems.* In: Adilson Rodrigues Pires and Heleno Taveira Torres (Organizers). **Principios de Direito Financeiro e Tributario: estudos em homenagem a Ricardo Lobo Torres**. pp. 319-344). Rio de Janeiro: Renovar, 2006.

GIARDINA, Emilio. ***Le Basi teoriche del principio della capacita contributiva***. Milan: Dottore Antonio Giuffre Editore, 1961.

GIARDINO, Cleber. Conflicts between tax on industrialized products and tax on operations relating to the circulation of goods. **Revista de Direito Tributario**, Sao Paulo, year 4, n. 13/14, p. 137-144, July/December 1980.

GRUPENMACHER, Betina Treiger. ICMS - considerations on the calculation basis. In: ROCHA, Valdir de Oliveira (Coord.). **Grandes questões atuais do direito tributario**. Sao Paulo: Dialdtica, 2006. v. 10, p. 18-38.

GUIMARAES, Maria Celeste Morais.**Recuperagao judicial de empresas e falência**. 2. ed. rev., atual. e ampl. Belo Horizonte: Del Rey, 2007.

HARADA, Kiyoshi. **Tax and Financial Law**. 14ª ed. Sao Paulo : Atlas, 2004.

KRAKOWIAK, Ricardo. **The principle of proportionality as a constitutional limitation on the power to tax**. Doctoral thesis. Sao Paulo: University of Sao Paulo Law School: 2005

LIMA, Persio de Oliveira. Hipotese de Incidencia do IPI.**Revista de Direito Tributario**, Sao Paulo, ano 3, n. 7/8,p. 191-197, jan./jun. 1979.

LORENZON, Gianfranco. *Scope of application.* In: Francesco Moschetti (coord.) - ***La capacita contributiva.*** (53-68). Padua: Casa Editrice Dott. Antonio Milani - CEDAM, 1993.

MACHADO, Hugo de Brito. **Tax Law Course**. 24th ed. Sao Paulo: Malheiros, 2004.

MANEIRA, Eduardo. The establishment of tax tariffs by Member States under the guise of tax substitution, in cases of acquisition of cell phones in other States of the Federation. In: MOREIRA, Andre Mendes; RABELO FILHO,Antonio Reinaldo; CORREIA, Armenio Lopes (Org.). **Direito das telecomunicagoes e tributagao**. Sao Paulo: Quartier Latin, 2006. p. 113-133.

. **Presumed calculation basis**. 2002. 238 f. Thesis (Doctorate in Tax Law) - Federal University of Minas Gerais Law School, Belo Horizonte.

. **ICMS - tax substitution**. Revista Dialetica de Direito Tributario, Sao Paulo, n. 95, p. 56-64, Aug. 2003.

MARTINS, Ives Gandra da Silva. Presumptions in tax law. In: MARTINS, Ives Gandra da Silva (Coord.) **Caderno de pesquisas tributarias**. Sao Paulo: Resenha Tributaria, 1984. v. 9.

MATTOS, Aroldo Gomes. ICMS: The Establishment of Tax Guidelines and Taxable Event without Provision in the Complementary Law. In: ROCHA, Valdir de Oliveira (Coord.). **Grandes questões atuais do direito tributario.** Sao Paulo: Dialetica, 2005. v. 9, p.11-27.

MELO, Jose Eduardo Soares de. **Social contributions in the tax system**. 5.ed. Sao Paulo: Malheiros, 2006b.

. ICMS - Calculation basis - Discounts, insurance, interest, fines, corrections, adjustments. Tariffs for tax substitution. Imports. Reduced Base and Credit Reversal. In: ROCHA, Valdir de Oliveira (Coord.). **Grandes questões atuais do direito tributario**. Sao Paulo: Dialetica, 2006a. v. 10, p. 276-301.

. **ICMS: theory and practice**. 10. ed. Sao Paulo: Dialetica, 2008.

. **ISS: theoretical and practical aspects**. 4. ed. rev. Sao Paulo: Dialetica, 2005. MINAS GERAIS. State Department of Finance. Minas Gerais Taxpayers Council. Agreement No. 19.765/10. Belo Horizonte, August 26, 2010. Minas Gerais, Belo Horizonte, September 25, 2010. Available at: <http://www.fazenda.mg.gov.br/empresas/conselho_contribuintes/acordaos/2010/3/19765103.pdf>. Accessed on: October 11, 2013.

. State Department of Finance. DOLT/SUTRI tax guideline no. 001/2008. Adjusted ST/MVA. Belo Horizonte, September 25, 2008. Available at: <http://www.fazenda.mg.gov.br/empresas/legislacao_tributaria/orientacao/orientacao_001_2008.htm>. Accessed on: October 11, 2013.

MINATEL, Josd Antonio. The concept of revenue for the purposes of PIS and COFINS. In: COELHO, Sacha Calmon Navarro (Coord). **Contributions to social security.** Sao Paulo: Quartier Latin, 2007. p. 527-548.

MORAES, Bernardo Ribeiro de. **Doctrine and practice of service tax.** Sao Paulo: Revista dos Tribunais, 1984.

NABAIS, Josd Casalta. **Por um estado fiscal suportavel: estudos de direito fiscal**. Coimbra: Almedina, 2005.

NUZZO, Enrico. ***Modelli rocostrutivi della forma del tributo,*** Padua: CEDAM, 1987.

OLIVEIRA, Josd Marcos Domingues de. **Tax law: ability to pay: content and effectiveness of the principle**. Rio de Janeiro: Renovar, 1998.

PAULSEN, Leandro. **Tax Law: Constitution and Tax Code in the light of doctrine and case law.** 5ª ed. Porto Alegre: Livraria do Advogado Editora, 2003.

PACHECO, Angela Maria da Motta. The legal tax recipient of the substantial tax obligation. In: Heleno Taveira Torres (coordinator), **Teoria Geral da Obrigação Tributaria: estudos em homenagem ao Professor Jose Souto Maior Borges**, (336/356). Sao Paulo: Malheiros, 2005.

PALAO TABOADA, Carlos. *El principio de capacidad contributiva como criterio de justiga tributaria: aplicacion a los impuestos directos e indirectos.* In: Heleno Taveira Torres (coord.), **Tratado de Direito Constitucional Tributario**, (285-304). Sao Paulo: Saraiva, 2005.

PONTES, Helenilson Cunha. **The principle of proportionality and tax law**. Sao Paulo: Dialbtica: 2000

QUEIROZ, Lrns Cesar Souza de. **Sujeigao passiva tributaria.** Rio de Janeiro: Forense, 1998.

REQUIAO, Rubens. **Commercial law course**. 26. ed. revised and updated by Rubens Edmundo

Requiao. Sao Paulo: Saraiva, 2005. v. 1.

REZEK NETO, Chad. **The principle of proportionality in the democratic state of law**. Sao Paulo: Lemos & Cruz, 2004.

SCHIAVOLIN, Roberto. *Il collegamento soggetivo.* In: Francesco Moschetti (coord.) - ***La capacita contributiva***(69/100). Padua: CEDAM - Casa Editrice Dott. Antonio Milani, 1993.

SIECKMANN, Jan-R. ***El modelo de los principios del derecho***. Colombian translation by various authors. Bogota: *UniversidadExternado de Colombia,* 2006, p. 13.

SILVA, Lrns Virgdio Afonso da. The proportional and the reasonable. In: **Revista dos Tribunais**, 798 (23-50). Sao Paulo: Apr. 2002.

. **Fundamental rights: essential content, restrictions and effectiveness**. Sao Paulo: Malheiros, 2009.

TIPKE, Klaus; LANG, Joachim. **Direito Tributario *(Steuerrecht),*** v.I. Brazilian translation of the 18th German edition by Luiz Doria Furquim. Porto Alegre: Sergio Antonio Fabris Editor, 2008.

. ***Moral Tributario del Estado y de los contribuintes (Besteuerumgsmoralund Steuer Moral).*** Translation, introduction and notes by Pedro M. Herrera Molina. Madrid: Marcial Pons, 2002.

. On the unity of the tax legal order. Brazilian translation by Luis Eduardo Schoueri. In: Luis Eduardo Schoueri e Fernando Aurelio Zilveti (coord.). **Direito Tributario: estudos em homenagem a Brandao Machado.** (60-70). Sao Paulo: Dialdtica, 1998.

TORRES, Ricardo Lobo. **Tratado de direito constitucional financeiro e** tributário, v. IV - Os tributos na Constituigao. Rio de Janeiro: Renovar, 2007, p. 46.

UCKMAR, Victor. **Common Principles of Constitutional Tax Law**. 2ª edition of the translation and notes by Marco Aurelio Greco. Sao Paulo: Malheiros, 1999.

About the author:

Marcelo Nogueira is a lawyer from the Pontificia Universidade Catolica do Rio de Janeiro, Master of Business Administration from Fundagao Getulio Vargas, and has taken several courses in Intellectual Property, Innovation and Tax Law at various national and international institutions (WIPO, Harvard Law School, Universe de Bordeaux, FGV, USP, UFRJ, etc.) throughout his 20-year career. He is the author of the book Dicas do Nogueira (2013) and of dozens of articles and interviews published in the main Brazilian news media, such as Jornal do Commercio, Jornal O Dia, Jornal O Globo, Radio CBN, Radio Justiga (STF), TV Globo, TV Futura, Consultor Juridico website, Migalhas website, Tribuna da Imprensa and others. He works as a consultant and expert at I&PI Consultoria em Inovagao e Propriedade Intelectual, as well as teaching courses, workshops and seminars.

MIX
Papier aus verantwortungsvollen Quellen
Paper from responsible sources
FSC® C105338

Printed by Books on Demand GmbH, Norderstedt / Germany